NORTH AMERICAN MOOSE

NORTH AMERICAN MOOSE

A Carolrhoda Nature Watch Book

by Lesley A. DuTemple

Carolrhoda Books, Inc. / Minneapolis

For Beth O'Brien, who's ventured into moose country with me for decades. With love and thanks for a wonderful friendship.

The author and publisher wish to thank Dr. Rolf Peterson and Candy Peterson for their assistance in the preparation of this book.

Text copyright © 2001 by Lesley A. DuTemple

Carolrhoda Books, Inc.
A Division of Lerner Publishing Group
241 First Avenue North
Minneapolis, MN 55401 U.S.A.

Website address: www.lernerbooks.com

LIBRARY OF CONGRESS CATALOGING-IN-PUBLICATION DATA

DuTemple, Lesley A.
    North American moose / by Lesley A. DuTemple
        p.   cm — (A Carolrhoda nature watch book)
    Includes index.
    Summary: Describes the physical characteristics, life cycle, and behavior of North American moose.
    ISBN 1-57505-426-4
    1. Moose—Juvenile literature. [1. Moose.] I. Title.
II. Series.
QL737.U55D86   2001
599.65'7—dc21   99-37091

Manufactured in the United States of America
1 2 3 4 5 6 – JR – 06 05 04 03 02 01

CONTENTS

THE BIGGEST DEER
IN THE WORLD

Most of the time, the great northern woods of North America are a peaceful place. Snowflakes drift over the landscape, spring flowers burst into bloom, and birds flit over sparkling brooks.

But every autumn, the quiet of the northern woods is shattered. The forest echoes with the sound of snorting. The ground shakes as massive hooves paw the earth. The very air crackles as enormous antlers clash. What causes this disturbance? The world's largest deer, *Alces alces*—the moose.

7

Moose are members of the deer family, which scientists call Cervidae (SUR-vih-dee). There are more than 60 **species,** or types, of deer living throughout the world. Five main species live in North America: mule deer, white-tailed deer, caribou, elk, and moose.

Moose have lived on our planet for thousands of years. They can be found throughout northern Asia, Europe, and North America. But many years ago, they lived only in Asia. How did they get across the Bering Strait, the body of water that separates Asia and North America? Moose are good swimmers, but they're not *that* good!

The moose's relatives include the caribou (above left), *the white-tailed deer* (left), *and the elk* (above).

8

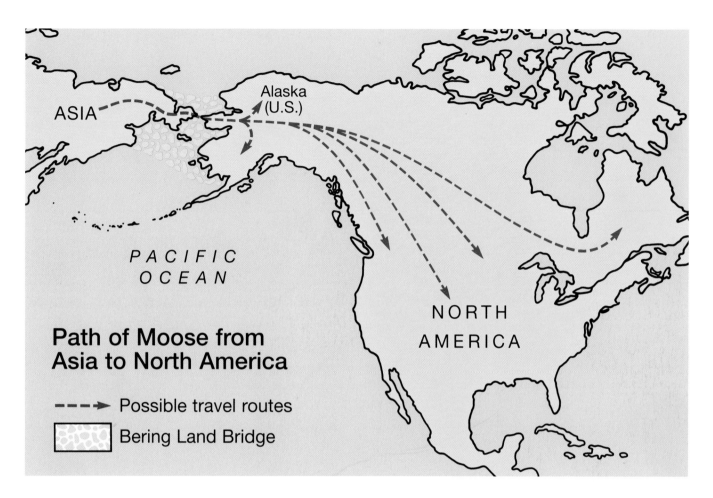

Path of Moose from Asia to North America

- - - -► Possible travel routes

▢ Bering Land Bridge

Moose were able to move onto the North American continent because Asia and North America were once connected by land. The Bering Land Bridge is a strip of land between Alaska and Siberia, a region in eastern Russia. About 2,000,000 years ago, temperatures dropped on many parts of the planet. Water that had been part of the oceans froze into huge sheets of ice. Without that water, the sea level dropped, and the Bering Land Bridge appeared.

Over the next 2,000,000 years, the bridge was covered by melting water, then revealed again by freezing, several times. Scientists think moose crossed the bridge between about 70,000 and 10,000 years ago. Then the ice melted, the sea level rose again, and the bridge disappeared under the waves once more. This time, the water didn't refreeze. The bridge is still there—it's just covered by water.

Scientists know that moose originated in Asia because they've found the oldest moose **fossils** there. Fossils are the remains of an animal or plant that lived thousands or millions of years ago. Moose fossils tell a strange story. Millions of years ago, the ancestors of the largest deer in the world were the size of a house cat! And they didn't yet have enormous antlers—they had tusks.

Over thousands of years, these animals' descendants gradually changed. By the time they moved from Asia to North America, they had gotten larger and lost their tusks. Their bodies continued to change as they learned to survive in their new home. In the process, they became the animals we recognize as moose.

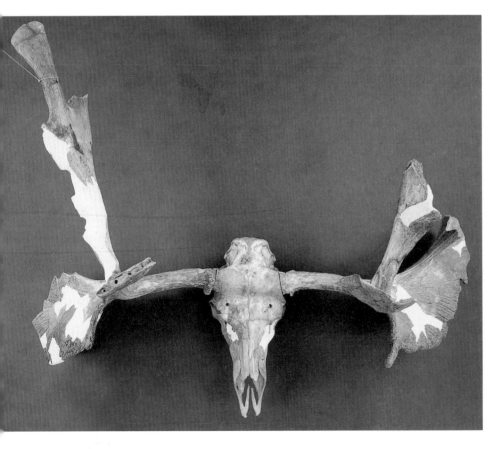

The fossilized skull and antlers of a stag-moose, an ancient relative of modern moose. Stag-moose died out about ten thousand years ago. This fossil was found in Canada's Yukon Territory.

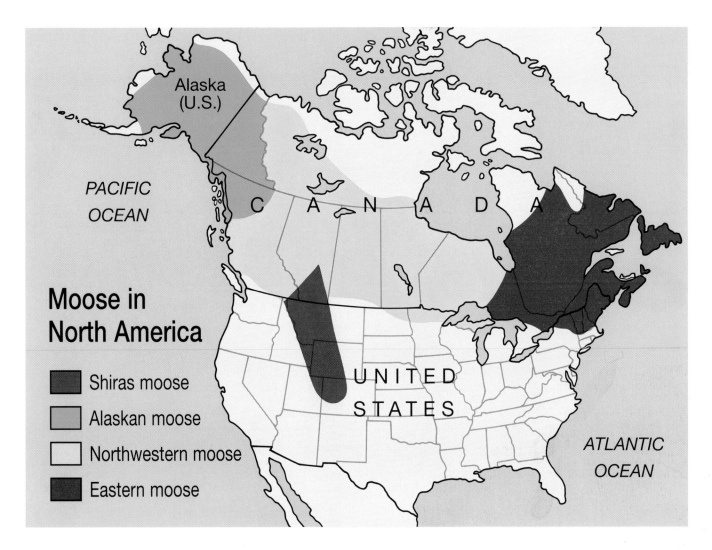

Moose in North America

- ■ Shiras moose
- ▨ Alaskan moose
- □ Northwestern moose
- ▦ Eastern moose

Throughout the world, moose are divided into seven subspecies. Four live in North America. They are the Alaskan *(Alces alces gigas),* the Shiras *(Alces alces shirasi),* the eastern *(Alces alces americana),* and the northwestern *(Alces alces andersoni)* moose.

Alaskan moose are found throughout Alaska and northwestern Canada. This is the coldest **range,** or living area, of any moose subspecies. Eastern moose live in the northeastern United States and eastern Canada. Shiras moose live throughout the Rocky Mountains of Colorado, Utah, Wyoming, Idaho, Montana, Alberta, and British Columbia. Northwestern moose live in northern Michigan, Minnesota, and North Dakota, as well as many parts of central and western Canada.

An Alaskan bull moose (left) *is bigger than an Alaskan cow moose* (below).

One difference between moose subspecies is size. A subspecies' size is determined partly by climate. The colder the climate, the bigger the moose. Scientists think that the extra size and weight help cold-climate moose stay warm enough to survive. A moose's size is also determined by its sex. **Bulls,** or male moose, are usually bigger than **cows,** or female moose.

Alaskan moose are the biggest subspecies of moose on Earth. An Alaskan bull moose may stand more than 7.0 feet tall (2.1 m)—and that's just to his shoulders, not including his head or antlers. An Alaskan bull standing under a basketball hoop would get his antlers tangled in the net. And the biggest Alaskan bulls weigh 1,800 pounds (820 kg)—about the same as a small car! Although cows are smaller than bulls, an Alaskan cow moose is usually bigger than a Shiras, eastern, or northwestern bull moose.

Eastern moose (above, in Ontario, Canada) and northwestern moose look very much alike. Some scientists consider them one subspecies, not two.

Eastern bull moose usually stand 6.1 to 6.4 feet tall (1.9–2.0 m) at the shoulder and can weigh more than 1,300 pounds (590 kg). Northwestern moose are about the same size. They're similar to eastern moose in other ways, too. In fact, some scientists think northwestern moose are so much like eastern moose that they don't consider the northwestern a separate subspecies. But a northwestern moose's palate, or roof of the mouth, is wider than the palate of an eastern moose and narrower than the palates of

Shiras and Alaskan moose. This is why some scientists consider the northwestern moose a separate subspecies.

The Shiras moose is the smallest subspecies. But it isn't small from a person's point of view. The largest Shiras bulls stand about 6.0 feet (1.8 m) at the shoulder and weigh about 1,200 pounds (540 kg). Shiras moose may be smaller than Alaskan moose because they live in a warmer, drier climate. Their winters are milder, so they don't need the extra bulk to survive.

This Shiras moose lives in Yellowstone National Park in Wyoming. Shiras moose are also called Yellowstone moose because so many live in the park.

The light brown color of this Alaskan cow's coat helps her blend into the open country she inhabits.

AT HOME IN THE HABITAT

All moose subspecies have hair that ranges from rust colored to very dark brown, almost black. So the color of a moose's coat won't tell you its subspecies, but it can tell you about its **habitat,** or the kind of environment in which it lives.

For example, an Alaskan moose that spends a lot of time in heavily shaded forests will have a very dark coat, while an Alaskan moose that spends more time in open, sunny country will usually be lighter in color. This color variation is an **adaptation,** or a change in response to living conditions, that helps moose survive. It's easier for animals to hide from danger if they blend well into the landscape.

Moose have adapted well to cold, snowy winters.

Moose habitat is a difficult place to live in. The winters are long and cold. For weeks, the temperature is below freezing, and the snow drifts higher than a person's head. But moose are adapted to the cold. Like many animals that live in cold places, they have an outer coat of rough, brittle, hollow hairs called **guard hairs.** Guard hairs are filled with air. When it's cold, they trap warm air next to the moose's body.

In winter, guard hairs grow longer and thicker. Moose also have another layer of fur to help them survive the cold. This fine, curly hair, called **underfur,** lies next to the skin, beneath the guard hairs. The underfur provides added protection from winter's icy blasts. On top of a moose's insulating guard hairs and underfur, fallen snow acts like an extra blanket, and the moose stays warm.

15

Summers in moose habitat may be wet and swampy, even hot. Clouds of biting insects fill the air. But heat and insects don't seem to bother moose as much as they do humans. When the insects are really annoying, moose go into the water. There, they can cool off in a safe spot where the bugs can't get to them.

A moose's guard hairs come in handy at this time of year, too. Since guard hairs are filled with air, they help moose stay afloat. In fact, moose are great swimmers. They've been known to swim 15 miles (24 km) without stopping.

Of all North American deer, only caribou can swim faster and farther than moose.

An Alaskan bull feeds on willow leaves in Denali National Park.

Besides cold winters and hot, buggy summers, every moose habitat has trees. Moose use trees for more than just shade or protection. Moose are **herbivores.** They eat trees and other plants.

Moose habitat has two types of trees. **Deciduous** (dih-SIHD-yoo-uhs) trees have leaves that fall off every autumn and grow back in the spring. Willows and aspens are deciduous trees. **Coniferous** (ko-NIHF-uhr-uhs) trees bear cones and usually have needles that stay green all year long. Pine trees are coniferous. In the winter, moose eat bark and pine needles because there's nothing else. But what they really like are willow leaves—a favorite moose food—and tender young tree branches.

17

A browsing bull

Moose need to eat a lot of leaves to stay alive. In the summer, an adult bull moose will eat about 60 pounds (27 kg) of plants every day! To get that much food, moose spend a lot of time browsing, or wandering and munching. They start early in the morning, take a break during the heat of the day, then browse again until dusk.

Moose have developed an efficient way of eating. They don't bite leaves off a tree. Instead, moose grab them with their **prehensile** upper lip. This upper lip is strong and flexible. It can seize and grasp things, much like a monkey's tail. To eat, a moose takes a branch in its mouth, wraps its upper lip around it, then pulls the whole branch sideways through the mouth. This action strips off all the leaves at once and gives the moose a big mouthful to chew.

But moose don't chew the way people do. In fact, they don't really chew at all. They don't have upper teeth in the front of their mouth—only lower teeth. A moose with a mouthful of leaves will just chomp it a few times, then swallow.

In addition to trees, any moose habitat has to have plenty of water. During the summer, moose spend a lot of time in water, usually eating **aquatic,** or water-dwelling, plants. Aquatic plants are rich in sodium, an essential mineral in a moose's diet. Most deciduous leaves are lower in sodium than aquatic plants. To stay healthy, a moose eats aquatic plants whenever they're available. It ducks its head underwater, wraps its upper lip around a plant stem, and yanks. If the plants are too deep to reach, the moose dives. A moose can dive to the bottom of an 18-foot (5.5-m) pond and come up with a plant in its mouth!

A Shiras cow feeds in a Wyoming pond.

Thanks to its four-chambered stomach, a moose can digest bark and spruce needles.

Although moose don't chew their food like humans do, their digestive system is well equipped to handle all the plants they swallow. Like all species of deer, moose are **ruminants.** Ruminants have stomachs with several, usually four, chambers.

After food is swallowed, it goes into the stomach's first chamber, where it is softened. Then the food is regurgitated, or brought up again into the mouth. This gives the moose a chance to chew the food again. At this stage, the food is called cud. Once the cud has been chewed, the moose swallows it again, and it passes through all four stomach chambers.

Moose need this extra stomach power because the plants they eat are especially hard to digest. Plants are made partly of cellulose (SELL-yoo-lohs), a woody fiber. The leaves and bark that moose eat have lots of cellulose. Humans eat plants all the time, but not the high-cellulose ones that moose eat. Our one-chambered stomach can digest lettuce and broccoli, but not leaves or bark.

20

Swampy ground doesn't bother moose. Their split hooves (inset, top right) *and dewclaws* (inset, bottom right) *help keep them from sinking.*

Because it's full of willow shrubs and water, moose habitat can be swampy and tangled. It's a hard place for humans to get around. But moose have adapted perfectly. Although they have enormous bodies and heads, moose have long, skinny legs. They look almost too fragile to support such a large animal. But those slender legs help moose move quickly and quietly, stepping over small shrubs and through big ones with ease. When necessary, moose can run short distances at 35 miles per hour (56 km/h) and trot for miles at 15 miles per hour (24 km/h).

Moose can even walk through swamps and bogs without sinking. Like all deer species, they have split, or two-toed, hooves. When a moose walks through a swamp, its toes spread slightly apart. The hooves widen, supporting the moose's weight the way snowshoes support a human walking on snow.

Moose also get support from their **dewclaws.** Dewclaws are two extra toes on the back of each foot, just above the hoof. If the ground is really mucky and the moose starts to sink, the dewclaws catch and spread out to keep the moose from sinking farther.

21

Although moose are comfortable in their habitat, they don't like sharing it with each other. Moose are solitary creatures. Other members of the deer family, such as elk, live in herds, or groups. But unless a few moose happen to gather to browse in a good feeding spot, they spend most of their lives by themselves. Moose tend to stay put, too, often remaining in the same area where they were born. They might travel a few miles as the seasons change to look for better food or a mate, but they're likely to do so alone.

Moose spend most of their days alone.

An Alaskan bull's remarkable antlers

FROM VELVET TO BONE

The most impressive feature of an adult bull moose is his antlers. Only bull moose grow antlers. Bulls produce a **hormone,** a chemical that causes changes in an animal's body, called testosterone. Scientists think that testosterone spurs antler growth.

Within the deer family, moose grow the largest antlers. Only the Irish elk had antlers larger than modern bull moose. An Irish elk's antlers were 11 feet wide (3.4 m) and weighed more than 100 pounds (45 kg)! But the last Irish elk died thousands of years ago. Some scientists believe the Irish elk died out because their antlers were so large. It was hard for the animals to move.

Mountain goats have horns, not antlers.

A bull's antler size varies depending on his subspecies. Alaskan moose, the largest subspecies, have the largest racks, or sets of antlers. An Alaskan bull's rack measures as much as 6.9 feet across (2.1 m) and weighs as much as 64 pounds (29 kg). Likewise, Shiras bulls—the smallest subspecies—have the smallest antlers. A Shiras bull's rack measures about 4 feet across (1.2 m) and weighs less than 40 pounds (18 kg). The racks of eastern and northwestern bulls are usually somewhere in between.

Many people confuse antlers with horns. Horns have a core of bone covered with keratin, the same protein found in your nails and hair. Animals that grow horns, such as cows, goats, and rhinos, usually grow only one set their whole life. The horns just get bigger every year.

Antlers are made of pure bone, just like the bones in your body. They're also deciduous. Like the leaves on a deciduous tree, antlers fall off near the end of every year and regrow every spring.

Antlers grow out of the top of a bull's head, just above his eyes. At first, the antlers are nothing more than knobs called **pedicles.** Each pedicle contains a "blueprint" for the antler. If a pedicle is damaged at this stage of growth, the antler will be deformed. And the same deformity may occur in each new set of antlers for several years. As the bull ages, the deformity usually disappears, leaving the moose with normal antlers.

The growing antlers are covered with fuzzy skin called **velvet.** Velvet contains blood cells and is covered with hair. It protects the antler and supplies nourishment as it grows. Velvet makes an antler look soft and furry—as if it were covered with velvet fabric. At this stage, the antlers are soft, fragile, and sensitive. They can be easily damaged, so bulls keep to themselves and try to avoid banging their antlers into anything.

Left: *Pedicles*
Above: *Antlers covered with velvet*

As velvet sheds, it often looks bloody. A bull's antlers are usually stained red for a while after the velvet has shed.

All spring and summer, the antlers grow. By early autumn, they've reached their full size for that year. The velvet is no longer needed, so it dries up and comes off in tatters. A bull at this stage looks like it has rags hanging from its antlers. The shedding velvet itches, so bulls rub their antlers against tree trunks, which helps the shedding process along. By this time, the antlers are no longer soft and fragile. They're hardened bone with points as sharp as knives.

Bull moose start to grow antlers when they're about 8 months old. The first antlers a bull grows are usually just spikes no bigger than a person's thumbs. But each year, the antlers grow back a bit bigger. The bull's second rack usually grows forked. The third, fourth, and fifth sets of antlers begin to look like smaller versions of a mature bull's antlers. They are palmated, or slightly flattened, with a few points, or prongs, on each antler.

A bull's first rack (above) *is just a pair of spikes. The antlers grow back a bit larger each year* (right).

A full-grown Alaskan bull with a large, palmated rack

As long as the bull stays healthy, for the next several years the antlers will grow back with more points and become more palmated. A bull's antlers are usually biggest when he's between 10 and 12 years old. After that, the antlers are a little smaller each year until he dies. Scientists think that the antlers may grow back smaller because at this age, the bull produces less testosterone.

Growing antlers takes a lot of energy. A bull has to be in good health and get plenty of nourishment to be able to grow a large rack. Why is antler growth worth expending so much energy? Scientists know of only one reason—the **rut.**

A Shiras bull scrapes a shallow hole as he tries to attract a mate.

FIGHTING IN THE FOREST

The rut occurs every autumn when bull moose fight each other for the right to mate with cow moose. Bulls are mature enough to mate when they are about 17 months old. But they don't usually mate until they are 5 or 6 years old, because they don't get a chance—the older bulls don't let them. Only the biggest and strongest bulls—those with the largest antlers—get to mate. Because sick and immature bulls can't mate, the next generation of moose has a better chance of being strong and healthy.

During the rut, bull moose are cranky. They lose interest in eating. They don't sleep much. The only thing that concerns them is finding a mate. To attract cows, some bulls dig a shallow hole in the ground, urinate, and wallow around in the urine. The scent attracts cows that are ready to mate. Cows also mark areas with their urine to attract bulls.

Two Shiras bulls compete for a mate.

Like bulls, many cow moose are mature enough to mate when they're about 17 months old. But they often don't mate until their third year. When a cow moose is ready to mate, she makes a mooing or moaning sound. Any nearby bull comes running when he hears that sound. He is prepared to fight anything that gets in his way as he tries to mate with the cow—especially other bulls.

If two bulls want to mate with the same cow, the bulls size each other up. They stare at each other and circle, comparing their antlers. Usually the smaller bull leaves quietly.

But sometimes the bulls are equally matched. Then they fight. The bulls step together, clash their antlers, and push. Sometimes they fight until one is killed or both are badly injured. But most of the time, one bull breaks off the attack, leaving the other to mate with the cow.

The cow and bull stay together for a few days. During this time, they may mate several times. Then they separate. After the bull departs, he may court other cows until the rut is finished, around the end of autumn. By December, most mature bulls have **cast,** or shed, their antlers. But you won't find many on the ground. Mice and other forest creatures eat them for the calcium and other minerals the antlers supply.

Scientists think that casting antlers helps bull moose get through the winter. Just as it takes a lot of energy to grow antlers, it takes a lot of energy to carry them. Winter is a difficult time for moose. Food is scarce and the weather is bad. If bulls had to carry their antlers through winter, many of them might not survive.

A mated pair of Shiras moose

An Alaskan cow with twin calves

A CALF IS BORN

Young moose, or **calves,** are born in the spring, when the weather is warmer than in winter and food is plentiful. Cows can have one, two, or three calves at a time. Usually they just have one. Twins are not uncommon, but triplets are rare.

A pregnant cow will seek out a quiet, safe spot to give birth. She tries to find a high spot on an island or a peninsula, a point of land surrounded by water on several sides. The cow does this because she needs to protect her calf and herself from **predators,** animals that hunt and eat other animals. Water makes it harder for predators to get to the cow and calf.

A newborn moose calf weighs about 35 pounds (16 kg). Calves look different from adult moose, and not just because they're smaller. Adult moose often have dark fur, but calves are born with pale brown fur. They spend a lot of time in sun-dappled thickets or grasses, so their lighter fur color helps them blend in with the background. A moose calf also has a shorter muzzle, or nose, than an adult. The calf's muzzle grows longer as the calf ages.

This Alaskan calf's light brown color helps it hide among shrubs and trees.

A cow stays close to her calf, watching for danger. Can you spot the cow's dewlap?

Calves are born without a **dewlap**. A dewlap is a flap of fur-covered skin that hangs from an adult moose's throat. It is sometimes called a bell or pendant. As the calf gets older, its dewlap develops.

When a calf is a few hours old, it can stand and walk a bit. Soon it can run and swim away from predators, but not as far or as fast as an adult moose. So the calf's mother stays close and guards the calf constantly.

A cow and her calf run for safety near the Kayukuk River in Alaska.

Cow moose are well equipped to protect their calves. Scientists aren't sure how well moose can see, but they know that moose have excellent senses of hearing and smell. An adult moose's long muzzle is full of nerve endings that enable it to smell things much farther away than any human could. Their ears can move independently—one ear can listen for sounds on the water while the other turns in the opposite direction and listens for sounds in the forest. So a cow can smell and hear a predator coming long before it arrives. Most of the time, she and her calf run away. But if they can't escape, the cow must be prepared to fight.

A cow moose with a calf is one of the most dangerous animals on Earth. She will charge at anything she thinks is a threat to her calf: wolves, bears, even humans and cars. If a predator comes near, the cow rears up on her hind legs and kicks the attacker with her hard, sharp front hooves. A moose can kill a wolf or bear this way.

Left: *A young calf gets nourishment from its mother's milk.*
Below: *After a few weeks, a calf's stomach is ready to digest plants.*

For its first few weeks, a calf gets food only by nursing, or drinking its mother's milk. A month-old calf can begin to eat plants. The cow teaches her calf everything it needs to know: what to eat, where to find water, and how to avoid and defend itself against predators. The cow even helps a tired calf swim by letting the calf rest its head and front feet on her back.

By the end of the summer, the calf stops nursing. As autumn begins, the cow is usually ready to mate again. She helps the calf survive its first winter while she is pregnant with her next calf. But when spring comes, the cow is ready to give birth. She pushes the **yearling,** or year-old calf, away and leaves it to start life on its own.

Sometimes the yearling doesn't want to go. It may try to stay near the cow even after her new calf is born. If the yearling gets too close to the baby, the cow will drive it away as if it were a predator. But when the new calf gets older, the cow sometimes lets the yearling stay with them.

Sometimes the first calf hangs around so long, it's still there when the mother pushes away the second calf. If this happens, the two half-siblings may browse and stay in the same area for a while. Generally, though, by the time a calf is a little over a year old, it will be on its own, living the solitary life of an adult moose. It may live as long as 20 years—unless it falls prey to one of the many dangers that moose face.

This Shiras yearling must survive the winter on its own.

This moose has fallen prey to a gray wolf.

PREDATORS AND OTHER DANGERS

A healthy adult moose doesn't have many natural predators. Wolves and bears prey upon moose, but a healthy adult is hard to catch. Its speed and strong senses of hearing and smell help it avoid most predators. If a predator does manage to get near, the moose can always rear up and kick with its front hooves. Wolves and bears are usually able to catch only sick, old, or very young moose.

In winter, though, even healthy adults can be caught if they get stuck in snow. Usually, a moose's long, slender legs enable it to walk through deep snow with ease. But sometimes a crust forms on top of the snow. The crust isn't strong enough to support a moose, but it's strong enough to support a wolf. The moose gets stuck, but wolves can run on top of the snow and attack it.

More frequently, it's not large predators that bring down moose. It's another type of deer—the white-tailed deer. The white-tailed deer is often infected by a **parasite** called a brain worm. A parasite is an organism, or life-form, that lives on or within a host organism. Parasites often damage their hosts. But brain worms usually don't do much damage to white-tailed deer.

Not so with moose. Where the ranges of white-tailed deer and moose overlap, moose become hosts to brain worms. Then they may develop a fatal disease called moose sickness. Infected moose often walk in circles or bump into trees because their eyesight and coordination are harmed by the brain worm. Sometimes their hind legs become paralyzed. Eventually, they die.

Winter ticks also cause problems for moose. Sometimes thousands of these ticks attach themselves to a single moose and spend the winter feeding on its blood. The problem is not the ticks themselves, but rather the itching they cause. To relieve this itching, a tick-infected moose scratches against shrubs and tree trunks. Sometimes the moose rubs its fur entirely off and scrapes its skin raw. Without its insulating winter coat and long guard hairs, the moose loses body heat. If the weather turns too cold, the moose may die.

This calf has moose sickness, a disease that can kill moose.

A Shiras cow and calf wade through deep snow to reach food.

Humans are also moose predators. Years ago, especially in the early 1900s, people killed too many moose. There were no rules about when people could hunt moose or which moose could be hunted. The moose population declined drastically. Although many states still allow moose hunting, rules control the number and type of moose people can kill, as well as the time of year hunting takes place.

But predators—whether big, little, or human—are not the greatest danger moose face. More moose die from starvation than any other cause. For large herbivores like moose, winter is a time of life-or-death struggle. Needles from coniferous trees are available for eating, but they don't provide as much nourishment as deciduous leaves and aquatic plants. Tree bark and sticks also provide little nourishment. All moose lose a lot of weight every winter. Many die.

Construction by humans has created new dangers for these moose.

Loss of habitat also creates problems for moose. When a shopping mall gets built in a willow meadow, or a marshy wetland is paved over for a parking lot, moose lose homes and food. And there's another habitat problem. Moose don't just try to avoid other moose. They don't like to live with humans, either. If humans move into moose habitat, the moose usually leave—even if the trees and aquatic plants are still there.

A scientist watches a moose from a safe distance on Isle Royale.

THE LIVING LABORATORY

For many years, scientists have been able to observe moose, their predators, and their parasites—along with the effects of habitat loss—all in one place. This "living laboratory" is Isle Royale, Michigan, an island and national park in Lake Superior.

In about 1910, a few moose managed to swim the 15 miles (24 km) between southern Canada and Isle Royale. Isle Royale was a moose paradise because no predators lived there—few bears or wolves can swim 15 miles. The moose had found a safe haven. Their population grew so well, scientists think that at one point there may have been more than 3,000 moose living on the 210-square-mile (540-sq-km) island. That's not much space for so many moose. Soon they ate most of the plants in their habitat, and many of the moose starved.

Then, in the winter of 1948, Lake Superior froze solid. A few wolves walked across the miles of ice to the island. When the ice melted, the wolves were stuck on Isle Royale with no way off—and a steady food supply. The moose population declined, and the island's plants began to grow back because there weren't as many moose to eat them.

For several decades, both the wolf and moose populations were stable. Then, in the early 1980s, a virus appeared on the island and attacked the wolves. Within two years, Isle Royale's wolf population went from 50 to 14. At one point, it dropped to 12.

A rare photograph of Isle Royale wolves. This picture was taken from an airplane.

An Isle Royale moose takes shelter in a thicket.

Although the wolf population has gradually recovered, it hasn't recovered at the same pace that the moose population has grown. By the summer of 1995, there were approximately 2,400 moose on the island, and the plants were once again disappearing. But by the spring of 1996, more than half of the moose were dead from starvation. Hard winters and wet, cold springs in 1997 and 1998 caused even more moose to die. In 1999, scientists counted 25 wolves and 750 moose.

Isle Royale is constantly changing. But for decades, it's been the best place on the planet to watch moose and their interactions with wolves, disease, and habitat loss. Scientists are always learning something new about this magnificent mammal of the North. Isle Royale is a closed environment, a place that other deer and their predators can't reach easily. So the data scientists gather there can't always be applied to moose that live in open wilderness areas, like Canada or Wyoming. But the information has still proved very useful.

The moose on Isle Royale face an uncertain existence, but what about other moose? About one million of the world's largest deer live in North America. That's a large population, but their future isn't secure. If we want the moose to remain a living, breathing animal, we need to preserve its habitat. And its habitat is wilderness.

Wilderness is land left to itself, land without human construction. No towns, no farms, no buildings, no highways. To survive, moose need the great expanses of wilderness found in the northern woods of North America.

Many organizations, such as the Nature Conservancy, the Audubon Society, and the Sierra Club, work hard to preserve large tracts of wilderness. The Nature Conservancy raises money to buy land and keep it as wilderness, while the Audubon Society and Sierra Club try to influence lawmakers to protect the environment. The United States and Canada also have national park systems that help preserve wilderness.

These efforts must continue. In saving wilderness, we do more than just preserve moose habitat. We preserve something that benefits all of us, from humans to moose to the tiniest parasite. We preserve our planet.

GLOSSARY

adaptation: a change in response to living conditions

aquatic: dwelling in water

bull: a male moose

calf: a young moose

cast: to shed antlers in autumn

coniferous: plants that grow cones. Coniferous plants usually have needles and stay green all winter.

cow: a female moose

deciduous: falling off every year, or having parts that fall off every year. A moose's antlers are called deciduous because they fall off at the end of autumn. Deciduous trees lose their leaves every year.

dewclaws: extra toes on the back of a moose's feet that help keep the moose from sinking on soft ground

dewlap: a flap of fur-covered skin that hangs from an adult moose's throat

fossil: the remains of a plant or animal that lived thousands or millions of years ago

guard hairs: rough, brittle, hollow hairs that help a moose stay warm and float in water

habitat: the type of environment in which an animal or plant normally lives

herbivores: animals that eat only plants

hormone: a chemical produced by an animal that can cause changes in its body

parasite: a life-form that lives on or within another life-form, often damaging it

pedicle: an antler in an early, knoblike stage of growth

predator: an animal that hunts and eats other animals

prehensile: able to bend and grasp objects

range: the area in which a type of plant or animal lives

ruminant: an animal with a multi-chambered stomach. A moose's stomach has four chambers.

rut: the period in autumn when male moose fight to mate with females

species: a type of plant or animal that has common traits, especially the means of producing young

underfur: the thick hair that grows next to a moose's skin

velvet: furry skin that contains blood cells and protects antlers as they grow

yearling: a year-old moose

INDEX

ABOUT THE AUTHOR

Lesley A. DuTemple makes her home at the edge of a canyon in Salt Lake City, Utah. She writes both books and magazine articles. Lesley is the author of another book in the Carolrhoda Nature Watch series, *North American Cranes.* She has also written four Early Bird Nature Books—*Whales, Tigers, Moose,* and *Polar Bears*—as well as *Jacques Cousteau,* all published by Lerner Publications. She is a regular contributor to *Dolphin Log,* the children's publication of the Cousteau Society.

Lesley is a graduate of the University of California. She did graduate studies for her M.B.A. at the University of Southern California. She lives with her husband, daughter, and son—as well as a dog, two cats, several tropical fish, a resident porcupine, a family of raccoons, and assorted deer.

The photographs in this book appear courtesy of: © Rich Kirchner/Rich Kirchner Wildlife & Nature Photography, front cover, pp. 19, 21 (left), 23, 29, 31, 36 (right), 37; © Beth Davidow/WorldWild Nature & Stock Photography, back cover, pp. 3-4, 12 (both), 14, 17, 20, 22, 24, 25 (right), 27 (top), 32, 33, 36 (left), 41 (top), 45; Visuals Unlimited: (© Patrick J. Endres) pp. 2, 6-7, 15, 28, (© Joe McDonald) pp. 8 (top left, bottom left), 25 (left), 38, (© Jack Ballard) p. 8 (right), (© Robert W. Domm) p. 13 (left), (© Forest W. Buchanan) p. 13 (right), (© Beth Davidow) p. 16, (© Glenn M. Oliver) pp. 18, 41 (bottom), (© Science VU) p. 21 (top right), (© George Herben) p. 21 (bottom right), (© Tom J. Ulrich) p. 26, (© Barbara Gerlach) p. 27 (right), (© Daniel D. Lamoreux) pp. 30, 40, (© Hugh Rose) p. 34, (© Natalie Abel) p. 35; Photographed by Harry Foster, 1981: reprinted with the permission of the Canadian Museum of Nature, Ottawa, Canada, p. 10; © Bill Peterson, p. 39; © Mary Hindelang, Ph.D., Wildlife Ecologist, Michigan Technological University, pp. 42-44. Maps on pp. 9, 11 courtesy of Laura Westlund.